I0795560

THRILLING THEME PARKS

UNIVERSAL STUDIOS

BY MONIKA DAVIES

EPIC

EPIC, AN IMPRINT OF BELLWETHER MEDIA BY FLUTTERBEE

EPIC BOOKS are no ordinary books. They burst with intense action, high-speed heroics, and shadows of the unknown. Are you ready for an Epic adventure?

This edition first published in 2027 by Bellwether Media, Inc.

Library of Congress Cataloging-in-Publication Data

Names: Davies, Monika author
Title: Universal Studios / Monika Davies.
Description: Epic. | Minneapolis, Minnesota : Bellwether Media, Inc, 2026. | Series: Thrilling theme parks | Includes bibliographical references and index. | Audience: Ages 8-12 | Audience: Grades 4-6 | Summary: ""Engaging images accompany information about Universal Studios. The combination of high-interest subject matter and light text is intended for students in grades 2 through 7"--Provided by publisher"-- Provided by publisher.
Identifiers: LCCN 2026011069 (print) | LCCN 2026011070 (ebook) | ISBN 9798898801069 library binding | ISBN 9798898802301 ebook
Subjects: LCSH: Universal Studios Florida (Orlando, Fla. : Amusement park) | Amusement parks--Florida | LCGFT: Juvenile literature
Classification: LCC GV1853.3.F62 D36 2026 (print) | LCC GV1853.3.F62 (ebook)
LC record available at https://lccn.loc.gov/2026011069
LC ebook record available at https://lccn.loc.gov/2026011070

Editor: Elizabeth Neuenfeldt Designer: Gabriel Hilger

Printed in the United States of America, North Mankato, MN.

TABLE OF CONTENTS

JUST LIKE THE MOVIES 4

THE MAKING OF UNIVERSAL STUDIOS....8

UNIVERSAL STUDIOS TODAY 16

UNIVERSAL STUDIOS EVENTS............. 20

GLOSSARY 22

TO LEARN MORE 23

INDEX 24

JUST LIKE THE MOVIES

Two friends sit in the Three Broomsticks. They share fish and chips. They feel like wizards from Harry Potter.

They raise their butterbeers. They grin. It has been a magical day at Universal Studios!

THREE BROOMSTICKS

BUTTERBEER

Universal Studios makes movies. It also runs **theme parks** around the world!

UNIVERSAL STUDIOS MAP

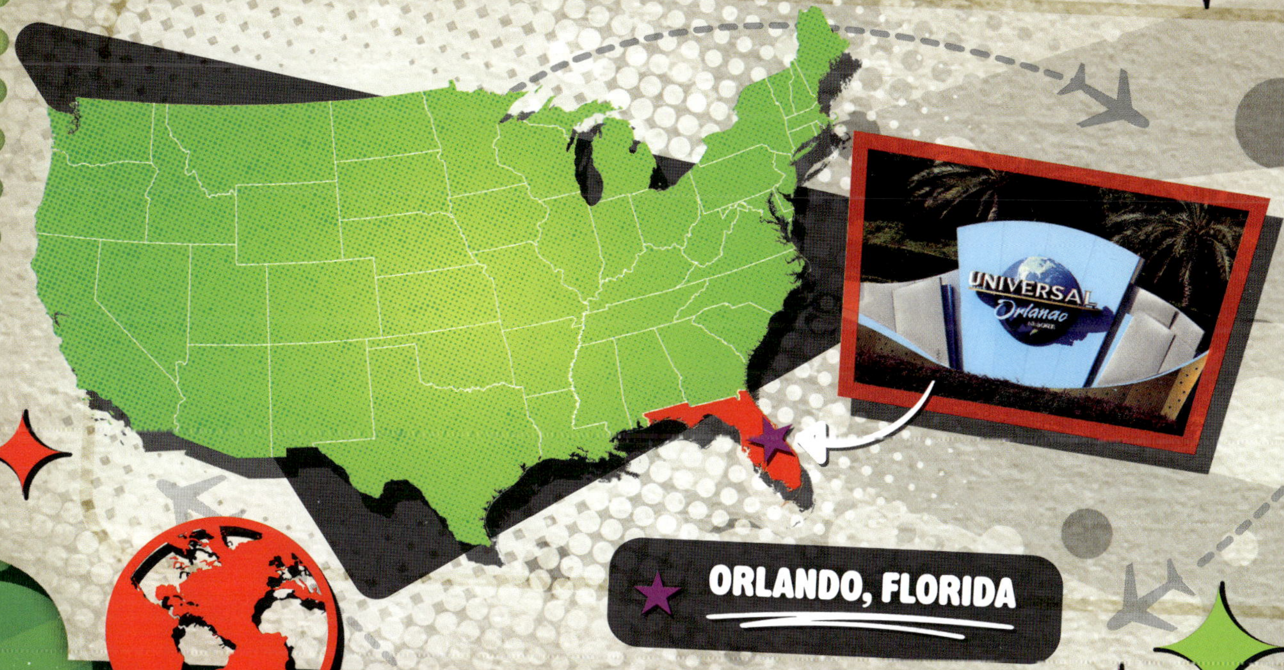

It owns six **resorts**. Universal Orlando Resort is its **flagship**. It is in Orlando, Florida.

THE MAKING OF UNIVERSAL STUDIOS

CARL LAEMMLE

BORN 1867

ROLE
Helped form Universal Pictures

ACCOMPLISHMENT
Opened film sets to the public in 1915

QUARTER TICKETS

Tour tickets were only 25 cents! That would be about $8 in 2025.

Universal Studios opened near Hollywood. Universal Pictures started making movies there in 1914.

Carl Laemmle helped form the studio. He opened film sets to the public. He wanted people to see filmmaking in action!

Universal Studios began its Studio Tour in 1964. Tour **trams** rolled through film sets.

Jaws came out in 1975. A *Jaws* section opened. A fake shark leapt out of the water!

FAMOUS SIGHTINGS

Steven Spielberg is a famous director. He made *Jaws*. He cut the park's opening day ribbon!

More **attractions** were added to the tour. But the studio had a dream. It wanted to build a large theme park.

The studio bought land in Florida. **Construction** began. Universal Studios Florida opened in 1990.

Universal Studios started small. There was only one theme park. It had 13 rides and shows.

But the studio kept adding new parks. Islands of Adventure opened in 1999. It has themed islands.

FLY WITH E.T.!

Most of the first rides are no longer at the park. But one is still open! Fans can still go on the E.T. Adventure ride.

Universal Studios Florida Attendance Records

UNIVERSAL STUDIOS TODAY

Universal Orlando Resort is big. It has four theme parks.

Volcano Bay is a water park. The main ride slides down a volcano! A Winding River allows visitors to relax.

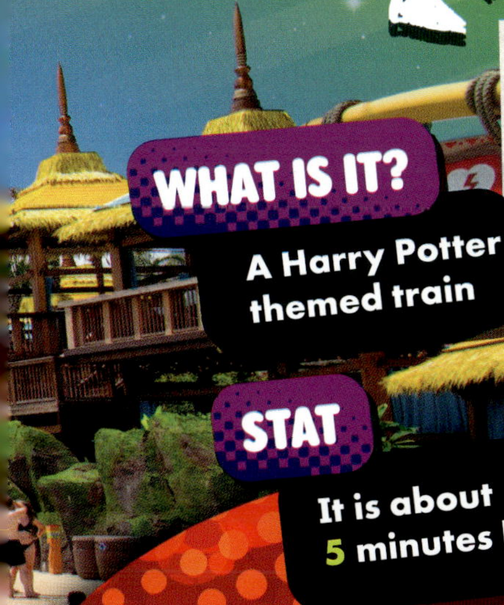

HOGWARTS EXPRESS

WHAT IS IT?

A Harry Potter themed train

STAT

It is about 5 minutes long.

FUN FACT

Riders see movie scenes.

SUPER NINTENDO WORLD

Epic Universe opened in 2025. It holds five worlds. Celestial Park is in the middle.

CELESTIAL PARK

Super Nintendo World is colorful. It puts people inside a video game! Dark Universe has monsters.

UNIVERSAL STUDIOS EVENTS

Mardi Gras is in February and March. Music plays. Street performers dance. Beads fly through the air.

Grinchmas

DATE

End of November to early January

LOCATION

Universal Orlando Resort

EVENT

Fans meet the Grinch and others in Who-ville.

Fans take home **souvenirs**.
Some buy wands. Others get toys.
Universal Studios is a fun time for all!

Glossary

attractions—interesting things that people want to see or visit

construction—the process of building something

flagship—the largest or most important of a group of things

resorts—places where people go for vacations

souvenirs—things people keep as reminders of places they visited

theme parks—parks where the rides and shows are based on a certain subject

trams—vehicles that run on tracks or rails and are often used to carry groups of people short distances

To Learn More

AT THE LIBRARY

Davies, Monika. *Walt Disney World.* Minneapolis, Minn.: Bellwether, 2027.

Downs, Kieran. *Super Mario Bros.* Minneapolis, Minn.: Bellwether Media, 2025.

Huddleston, Emma. *Harry Potter.* Minnetonka, Minn.: Kaleidoscope, 2020.

ON THE WEB

FACTSURFER

Factsurfer.com gives you a safe, fun way to find more information.

1. Go to www.factsurfer.com.
2. Enter "Universal Studios" into the search box and click .
3. Select your book cover to see a list of related content.

Index

attendance, 15

attractions, 4, 10, 11, 12, 18, 19

Grinchmas, 20

Hogwarts Express, 17

Laemmle, Carl, 8, 9

map, 7

rides, 14, 17

theme parks, 6, 12, 13, 14, 16, 17, 18, 19

The images in this book are reproduced through the courtesy of: Mia2you, front cover, pp. 1, 16; ADVTP, front cover, p. 1; Chizhevskaya Ekaterina, front cover, p. 1; Imago/ Alamy Stock Photo, front cover, p. 1; veritographer, pp. 2-3, 18-19; Hannari_eli, p. 3; Mathew Monteith/ Alamy Stock Photo, p. 4; Solarisys, pp. 5, 15 (attendance); Julien-images-videos-93, p. 5 (butterbeer); Wangkun Jia, p. 6; Katherine Welles, p. 7; PictureLux/ The Hollywood Archive/ Alamy Stock Photo, p. 8; Heritage Image Partnership Ltd/ Alamy Stock Photo, p. 8 (inset); Masheter Movie Archive/ Alamy Stock Photo, p. 9; Bob Riha Jr/ Contributor/ Getty Images, p. 10; ullstein bild Dtl./ Contributor/ Getty Images, p. 11; Nick Ut/ AP Images, p. 12; NBCUniversal/ Wikimedia Commons, p. 13; Craig Russell, pp. 14, 21; Steven Miller/ Wikimedia Commons, p. 14 (inset); Robert Linsdell/ Wikimedia Commons, p. 15 (Islands of Adventure sign); Wayne Hacker/ WarrenImages.com/ Alamy Stock Photo, p. 15 (Islands of Adventure); bella1105, p. 17 (Hogwarts Express); Paula Montenegro Stock, p. 17 (sign); Sipa USA/ Alamy Stock Photo, p. 19 (Celestial Park); Inside the Magic/ Flickr, p. 20.